Man Made by Grace

By: Willie Deeanjlo White
Servant; Father; Son; Pastor

Copyright ©2019 Willie Deeanjlo White by (Higher Ground Books & Media)
All rights reserved. No part of this publication may be reproduced may be reproduced in any form, stored in a retrieval system, or transmitted in any form, or by any means (electronic, mechanical, photocopying, recording or otherwise) without prior permission by the copyright owner and the publisher of this book.

Scripture taken from the HOLY BIBLE, New King James Version ®. NKJV®. Copyright 1979, 1980, 1982 by Thomas Nelson. All rights reserved worldwide.

Higher Ground Books & Media
Springfield, Ohio.
http://www.highergroundbooksandmedia.com

Printed in the United States of America 2019

Man Made by Grace

By: *Willie Deeanjlo White*
Servant; Father; Son; Pastor

Table of Contents

DEDICATION

Introduction

The sharpening

    a. The File

    b. The Whetstone

    c. The Sandpaper

Countenance - The Stages of Manhood becoming God Centered

Bible Resource Reference

Resource Reference

DEDICATION

This Book is Dedicated to my loving family who are always my supporters. A special shout out to J. Marcell, Jeannine and Richard White.

Introduction

Proverbs 27:17 Iron sharpeneth iron; so a man sharpeneth the countenance of his friend.

Proverbs 27:17 Iron sharpens iron; So, a man sharpens his friend's countenance.

17 As iron sharpens iron, so a friend sharpens a friend.

In looking at the concept of Iron Sharpening Iron as it relates to the process of manhood, I am perplexed. I have always been taught that the Bible never contradicts itself and that everything in the Bible is true. Every Word that proceeds out of the Mouth of God is factual and the Bible is the Living Word of God. I know all of this to be true and have in time tried it over and over and have always come back to the fact that the Bible is the one true source of irrefutable inspiration from God. I am not talking about challenging scientific experiences, but I am talking about in my life. Because of this fact, the concept of iron sharpening iron is perplexing, I have learned that it takes a harder metal to actually sharpen iron than iron, so the concept of trusting the Word in this example makes me look at it deeper and deeper thus causing my thoughts to be propelled.

I think that is the true meaning of a Proverb in general and it is not a coincidence that I find my quandary in a book that is known for its complexities or I should say, known for its mysterious truths. The Book of Proverbs for me is a book of helpful guidelines, birthed out of a supernatural wisdom that had to come from a supernatural source to be released in a way that requires a person to find their own truth in the message.

In this Book I have found justification for my actions and freedom from mistakes. As I reared my son, I took comfort in the fact that I was told to whip his behind.... Proverbs 23:13 Withhold not correction from the child: for if thou beatest him with the rod, he shall not die. But not just because I wanted to whip him, but the book of Proverbs also gives meaning and purpose to the process which I am glad to say matched up with my motives which were always love, Proverbs 13:24 He that spareth his rod hateth his son: but he that loveth him chasteneth him betimes.

It was these types of truths that help to increase my faith not only in God's Words ability to guide me in the day to day process of raising my son, but it is also in His Word that I find futuristic confidence in His promises as well for He also says in Proverbs 22:6

Train up a child in the way he should go: and when he is old, he will not depart from it. It is in that truth that I currently hold onto to see the fruition of His promise to me.

So, it is with that train of thought and position of hope that I take this journey into this new endeavor mandated to me from above. I will ask God to guide me through this process of taping into my life's experiences to further develop the concept of men helping men.

Father God I surrender myself to You and trust Your Word in my spirit and humbly submit to Your call in my life today.

Chapter One

The Sharpening

Proverbs 27:17 Iron sharpeneth iron; so a man sharpeneth the countenance of his friend.

In my pursuit of getting a better understanding of the sharpening process, it became clear to me very quickly that the concept or iron sharpening iron was not scientifically sound. In order to sharpen a piece of iron, a harder metal is required to do the job. Iron would not sharpen iron, it would only cause friction if rubbed together resulting in both blades becoming heated, but not producing any substantial improvements in the blades ability to cut.

To sharpen according to dictionary dot.com means, "to make or become sharp or sharper.", and the word sharp has several meanings that I will explore a little further, I am only listing those definitions that I want to explore.

Sharp is defined as:

1.having a thin cutting edge or a fine point; well-adapted for cutting or piercing: *a sharp knife.* 3.involving a sudden or abrupt change in direction or course: *a sharp curve in the road; The car made a sharp turn.* **6.** clearly defined; distinct: *a sharp photographic image.* **7.** distinct or marked, as a contrast: *sharp differences of opinion.* **11.** felt acutely; intense; distressing: *sharp pain.* **12.** merciless, caustic, or harsh: *sharp words.* **13.** fierce or violent: *a sharp struggle.* **14.** keen or eager: *sharp desire.* **15.** quick, brisk, or spirited. **16.** alert or vigilant: *They kept a sharp watch for the enemy.* **17.** mentally acute: *a sharp lad.* **18.** extremely sensitive or responsive; keen: *sharp vision; sharp hearing.* **19.** shrewd or astute: *a sharp bargainer.*

To make sharp and sharp being for the initial purpose a thin cutting edge, iron sharpening iron is a concept that just does not match. In fact, in order for an iron blade to become sharp or to have a thin cutting edge, it requires a threefold process, involving a file, a stone and sand paper.

Looking at the idea of iron being symbolic of a man, this concept gives a different meaning to the other definitions for sharp in reference to a man being able to be a positive asset to another man. Sometimes in life, it will require you to make some sudden abrupt changes in the direction of your life that can be better defined by someone who has already been there. Their personal experience will help to give you a clearer picture of the path that you will have to take. If the experiences are properly applied, then that viewpoint will help to lessen the intensity and distress of the journey thus reducing the culture shock that is sometimes perceived as pain.

The information from others is not always delivered in a subtle manner and can even be interpreted as merciless, or harsh which is in direct contrast to the intended purpose. But the struggles faced by most will require a fierce violent type of passion that can only be birthed by a keen and eager energy that must be maintained by an alert and vigilant mental acuteness that sometimes can only be developed in an atmosphere of extreme responsiveness. When to apply pressure and when to apply tack is most effective when the sharpener is shrewd.

Back to the process of sharpening iron as a metal I think we will further be able to draw from this symbolic reference to man. The threefold process of sharpening iron as defined by William Jackson and ehow.com as follows:

The File

- The iron object--typically a blade of some sort--is propped up on a support. This support could be a small wooden block, a stone or anything else that can lift up one side of the blade an inch or two off of the ground. A standard metal file is then used, set at about a 30- to 35-degree angle, to file the edge of the blade. The filing is typically done in slow, measured strokes until a rough, sharp edge has been revealed on the blade. Since iron is softer (more malleable) than steel, only a handful of file strokes are needed. Once the sharp but roughened edge has been revealed all along the edge of the blade, the filing phase is finished.

Whetstone

- The filing phase of the iron sharpening has revealed a rough edge--rough because it has created tiny protrusions of iron. A little oil is now applied to a whetstone and the iron blade is rubbed against it, back and forth. The hardness of the whetstone crushes up against the tiny protruding metal bits and rubs them off, leaving a smooth, sharpened and polished edge to the iron blade.

Sandpaper

- The final phase when it comes to iron sharpening is the sandpaper phase. Heavy-duty sandpaper is rubbed, extremely carefully, along both sides of the iron blade's edge. The sharpener must take care not to cut his fingers during this process. The sandpaper helps to blend the edge with the rest of the blade while adding an extra and final touch of sharpness.

Let's start with the File

The File

- The iron object--typically a blade of some sort--is propped up on a support. This support could be a small wooden block, a stone or anything else that can lift up one side of the blade an inch or two off of the ground. A standard metal file is then used, set at about a 30- to 35-degree angle, to file the edge of the blade. The filing is typically done in slow, measured strokes until a rough, sharp edge has been revealed on the blade. Since iron is softer (more malleable) than steel, only a handful of file strokes are needed. Once the sharp but roughened edge has been revealed all along the edge of the blade, the filing phase is finished.

The iron object in this case is a man is propped up on a support. In the process of preparing the blade to be correctly positioned to be sharpened it is important to understand that the blade will have to lean on something, it will need assistance assuming the position. It is not always easy to get into the position and God will sometimes use some uncommon events to get you where He needs for you to be.

The blade needed to be propped and what it was propped up on was not really significant. It "could be a small wooden block, a stone or anything".

Now it was not as important of what the support was, but what the support could do. The support has to be able to lift the blade up off of the ground an inch or two. In the concept of a man sharpening a man this example is saying that it is not as important who you chose to assist you, but it is absolutely relevant that they be able to lift you…as with Moses in the wilderness. God could have told anybody to hold up the hands of Moses to give victory to His people, but he chose two people close to the struggle, two people who knew the man Moses. As the people of God battled the Amelek it was clear that as long as Moses held up his hands they would win, but when his hands came down, they would start to lose. So, Aaron Moses' brother and Hur one who had traveled with them sat Moses down on a rock so that they could be in the correct position to be able to hold up his arms without their arms becoming tired. With the proper preparation they were able to hold his arms up until the sun went down and the battle won. "Exodus 17:12 But Moses' hands were heavy; and they took a stone, and put it under him, and he sat thereon; and Aaron and Hur stayed up his hands, the one on the one side, and the other on the other side; and his hands were steady until the going down of the sun."

There was another significant event where a man needed help to hold something up to be able to fulfill His destiny. As they led Christ to His Crucifixion a man was chosen to assist Him with carrying the Cross. Matthew 27:31-32 And after that they had mocked him, they took the robe off from him, and put his own raiment on him, and led him away to crucify him. And as they came out, they found a man of Cyrene, Simon by name: him they compelled to bear his cross. And in Mark 15:20-21 And when they had mocked him, they took off the purple from him, and put his own clothes on him, and led him out to crucify him. And they compel one Simon a Cyrenian, who passed by, coming out of the country, the father of Alexander and Rufus, to bear his cross. And in Luke 23:26 And as they led him away, they laid hold upon one Simon, a Cyrenian, coming out of the country, and on him they laid the cross, that he might bear it after Jesus. And John says in John 19:17 And he bearing his cross went forth into a place called the place of a skull, which is called in the Hebrew Golgotha:

In the dramatizations of the event we often see a depiction of Jesus and Simon dragging a cross through the streets, with Christ being beaten and tattered to the point of exhaustion needing the assistance of another to help Him complete his journey and once again anybody could have done it, but Simon was that man in the crowd first capable of the task and is one who is suspected to have had been a Jew and thus being one of His own people.

Too many times when we are looking for help, we tend to look outside of our own. It is easier to ask a stranger for help, than it is for a man to become vulnerable with another male from his own house, club, inner circle or Church. Even though the exact male needed for the job is at times unknown, we know the task at hand will require a certain kind of support that is best found from someone who can understand the reality of the struggle.

During the File process the block or leaning object is only an object needed to raise the blade off the ground to create the 30 to 35-degree angle. The correct angle is needed in order to prepare the blade to go through a process designed to bring out its true purpose. The File is needed to accomplish this process because steel is a harder metal then iron.

One of the biggest mistakes men often make when attempting to deal with life's issues is to turn to a woman for support because of her more nurturing nature. But in true reality if he is ever going to achieve his purpose, he will need something harder than he is to bring out his true potential and that toughness will never be found in a woman. One of the biggest attacks of Satan on the family is to remove the father from his post. In just about every negative subset of the culture i.e. prison populations, homelessness, drug addictions and such, one commonality is almost always consistent regardless of race and that is the absence of a consistent Father in the home. Men need men to become men….

In the File process, "The filing is typically done in slow, measured strokes until a rough, sharp edge has been revealed on the blade." Filing is the rubbing of the steel file across the iron blade. The file itself has a special property that makes it perfect for the job. Not only is the file made of a harder metal, but the design of the file is as such to create a special type of reaction when rubbed against the blade. The file is typically made in a round or triangle pattern with a series of horizontal ridges and groves from the handle to the end of the length of the tool. These ridges and grooves where designed to purposefully cut into or cut away the outer layer of the blade to be sharpened. The slow measured strokes are the most efficient and effective way to accomplish the process, but in the hands of a novice a more erratic procedure might be applied thus yielding an uneven result.

As the file is rubbed against the blade in the correct angle enough of the iron will be cut away leaving a revealed cutting edge. This edge is able to accomplish the job of cutting certain things but without completion of the sharpening process, at this phase the iron blade will create a raggedy tear in the object to be cut.

It is important to not judge those individuals God has placed in your path. As with the unique design of the file, each man has a unique pattern of growth. We all can't be triangles or round. Each one has his own set of grooves and cross patterns that have been carved out by his own experience, but each one of those grooves has the ability to reveal some things that you did not know were hidden.

As I look at one of the men God placed in my path, I can remember my initial impression of him was that we were not going to get along. He was pushy, opinionated and somebody that thought he knew everything. He also was a stickler for being on time, one of those folks who believed that if you are on time you are already late kind of folks. He was older, blacker, meaner and at times louder than me. I later learned that he came from the Jehovah's Witness Church and that made him even less appealing to me.

As I reflect, I can remember that each one of his trials that developed the different groves that I sometimes classified as flaws were used by God to develop some sort of character strength in me. His constant attention to my coming and going by the not so gentle tapping of his watch when I arrived produced time awareness. His surprise scripture drills that he was taught as a witness developed in me that openness to look deeper at a passage of scripture to glean a deeper meaning. Those assignments to be early to open the building or to stay late to close and lock up the building developed commitment and patience characteristics that I lacked. I could go on and on about the individuals and their perceived issues that God used to build strengths in me, but I will say that as with the sharpening process the trick was in the slow methodical delivery of the strokes and the consistent application of pressure applied was needed and if any one of the files God chose to use had moved to quickly, I would have bulked even more.

Paul often times refers to those he was grooming in the Bible as his Son's and in the process, they were being developed or sharpened into the tool God intended for them to become. Those sons would go on to be the founders of many of the early churches. Once the filing is complete then there is a sharpness that is revealed that is raw and unstable. If the man is not careful at this point he will be tempted to run off half-cocked and do his own thing, but just like in the case of the sharpening process the result of anything he attempts to cut i.e. cut out his carrier, cut out his family direction, cut out his ministry, cut out his identity, cut out his goals, will be raggedy.

Now we will examine the Whetstone

The Whetstone

- The filing phase of the iron sharpening has revealed a rough edge--rough because it has created tiny protrusions of iron. A little oil is now applied to a whetstone and the iron blade is rubbed against it, back and forth. The hardness of the whetstone crushes up against the tiny protruding metal bits and rubs them off, leaving a smooth, sharpened and polished edge to the iron blade.

During and after the filing phase of the sharpening process the blade begins to look worse than it did before the process began. No matter if the blade was just being forged from the fire or folded in a process similar to or as thorough as the ancient art of Japanese metal folding to create a superior blade, the dull edge that is left appears just that dull. I liken that dullness to the look in the eyes of that wandering child of God that has been newly converted and is just not sure what to do or how to act, although his reactions are slowed and unsure, in some operations he can be quite useful. The unfinished blade of a knife can cut, but in most cases, they are not very efficient and depending on the thing being cut, might even be ineffective and cause a ragged tear.

As the file has rubbed against this surface…it has ripped it up in places and roughened others. The appearance of the blade is in some areas minimally intrusive if not outright raggedy. As God uses the Pastor, the Elders, the Deacons and Brothers both young and old as a file sometimes the reaction by the young convert is sharp, raggedy and even harsh. He may go through periods of being out right rude and discontent, after all no one likes being bruised. Thank God we serve a willing God for the Bible tells us in Isaiah 53:5 that our savior will be wounded for our transgressions and bruised for our iniquities and through the torture of the scourging, through the humiliation of humanness, through every scar, whelp and tear or as it is written through His stripes we are healed. So, we have to learn some patients with each other as God does what He is doing through others in the lives of others. We have also got to learn to be patient with ourselves as we are uncomfortable with our reactions or revealed protrusions through the process.

Now let's look at the whetstone…on the surface it is pretty self-explanatory. The directions say apply some oil to the whetstone and apply the blade to the stone, rubbing back and forth to polish. Well in my research I discovered some very fascinating facts about the process. First of all the Whetstone itself, needs no oil. The term whet according Dictionary.com means to sharpen; the word stoning means, "to rub something with or on a stone, as to sharpen, polish or smooth". When you put the two terms together you not only have a word that resembles the act but also a word that possesses the total instructions needed for the act. Whet to sharpen and the Stoning is the how to sharpen.

But just like other principles of God, man has in his attempt to understand the word; he has applied human principles across the board. Because it sounds like something, he understands then instead of pursuing the God intended purpose of a thing he has added his understanding of physicists to it so it has to apply. Often times in looking at a thing it is easier to assume then to believe. God said His understanding is above our understanding, and to truly understand His intentions in a thing it always requires faith.

The Whetstone has everything needed to complete its phase of the conversion process, just like those assigned to you will have everything needed to complete their purpose in your life. In the

Church we symbolically use types of oil in the process of prayer that represents the anointing of God. This process is not just a tradition of religion but the use of oil was ordained of God in the consecrating of the Most Holy of Holies. A special formula for the type of oil to be used in the consecrating process was given to Moses in Exodus 30:34-36. A lot of people confuse that oil with the oil used our Church services. The oil used in our services is more in alignment with the meaning of the oil used by Jacob when he realized he was in a place of God or a House of God. In the first mention of oil in the Bible in Genesis 28:18 which states, "And Jacob rose up early in the morning, and took the stone that he had put for his pillows, and set it up for a pillar, and poured oil upon the top of it." Jacob poured the oil on the stone that he had rested on as he wrestled with God to mark the place as a Holy place. He also renamed the reign calling it Beth-el or House of God…just because you live in the same place or work at the same place or have to stay in the same circumstances does not mean that God cannot change it for you. There is a lot of confusion about Luz and Beth-el and were they two distinct places…well for me it is clear, Jacob had a personal encounter with God in a place called Luz that he chose to call Beth-el because of the overwhelming presence he felt there. Anytime the presence of the Lord is heavy then that place is marked, and others will take notice, and over time we forget Luz and God's House will always stand. So no matter how you got to the House of God always remember that just like Jacob's experience, yours has the ability to change other's opinion of where you came from.

Just like that first use of Oil in the Bible was to mark the place of recognition of the presence or House of God the oil applied to the Whetstone symbolizes our recognition of the need for God's presence and help in this process. No the stone itself does not require any oil, but the person assigned to be your stone does. If the person who is pouring into you is not saved then he cannot tap into the oil of God on your behalf. The Whetstone has a specific design for a specific purpose and so do those who God assigns to your life.

One remarkable noticeable difference in the Whetstone phase of the Sharpening process is the direction of the pressure. In the filing process the file is applied to the blade, but in the Whetstone phase the blade is applied to the stone, "A little oil is now applied to a whetstone and the iron blade is rubbed against it, back and forth. The hardness of the whetstone crushes up against the tiny protruding metal bits and rubs them off" in this phase of the process it will require **You** to do more of the work. Understanding that those assigned to you can take it…if they could not then they would not be there. Sometimes you will have to open up and share some ugly truths about yourself, sometimes you will have to show up early and stay late to be able to get what God has for you in a situation. I remember when we first moved into our new building, I was told to be at church an hour earlier than service and had to stay until everyone was gone to secure the building. Now I did not have to actually do anything but show up and watch one of the Pastor's do it, but I was required to be there. I could not understand why week after week I had to be there, I did not understand why I was not given a key to unlock the building since I was often times there first, I did not understand why the only thing I was allowed to do was walk around and shake the doors despite my having knowledge of how to do a lot more, but I trusted God. Today I can see that during that process not only was I acquiring an appreciation for what Pastor does, but I was being provided patience, humility and respect, that I needed. I was raised to respect but being told to respect is a lot different than actually showing respect. Arrogance, independence, control and know it all ism were just a few of the those protrusions revealed in me by the filing process, but as I got busy doing the work of God even before I knew what that was, God began through many men to rub away things that made me less affective for Him.

The goal of the Whetstone is to leave a smooth, polished and sharpened edge…Thank God for shining me up. No, I am not perfect, but in His polishing of me I can be useful for Him…. Hear that Useful for Him. The Whetstoning process takes as long as it does…don't get frustrated during the change. Remember the Bible teaches us in Ecclesiastes 9:10, "Whatsoever thy hand findeth to do, do it with thy might; for there is no work, nor device, nor knowledge, nor wisdom, in the grave, whither thou goest." It is not as important what work you do in this phase but get busy. Trust those who are assigned over you to guide you, but don't get all caught up in what the job is.

A brother approached me to stand in the doorway to greet, and then to monitor the parking lot during service, then to provide security inside the service. While being on post, I was approached, by a sister, to pray for the services on a prayer team. While working on security and functioning on the intercessor team I was able to hear the voice of God as he called me into ministry. I was then assigned to the various meetings and groups to be prepared for ministry and in one of those sessions, God placed me on the heart of one of the Elder's to be assigned to Baptism. My first assignment was to watch, pray and clean which opened me up to a level of helps where I began to care for the Baptismal clothing and supplies. I was approached by the director of the Tarry Room and pulled into that training which is customarily called the second part of the Baptism but could actually happen first if God says so. But in that training I was further taught and developed spiritually as I also attended the second level ministerial classes and required alliance meetings to further connect with the Body…. all of this took place before moving to the new building and being told to show up early…and wait. The Whetstone process is an ongoing process and one that God will reuse every time one of those imperfections rears its ugly head in your life.

Lastly, we will look at The Sandpaper

The Sandpaper

- The final phase when it comes to iron sharpening is the sandpaper phase. Heavy-duty sandpaper is rubbed, extremely carefully, along both sides of the iron blade's edge. The sharpener must take care not to cut his fingers during this process. The sandpaper helps to blend the edge with the rest of the blade while adding an extra and final touch of sharpness.

In the sandpaper phase of the sharpening process it is very important that the person using the sandpaper is skilled and even in that he must be careful. This leaves room for continued growth and improvement, not only in the condition of the blade, but also in the skill set of the sharpener. At this point in the process the individual will for all intense and purposes appear complete. When you look at a knife that needs sharpening, sometimes you don't really know that it is dull until you attempt to use it. Now the blade does not become dull by being inactive itself, in fact the blade can only lose its edge by being used. The only way you can pull a dull knife from a drawer is the last person who used it did not take the time to care for it properly before putting it away. In the process of working in the Kingdom of God it is often times the process where a person will become tired and ineffective because of poor personal or systemic care. Thank God that He tells us to not become weary in our well doing and to faint not because in the end He promises to add increase to your lack. In Galatians 6:9 the Bible says, "And let us not be weary in well doing: for in due season we shall reap, if we faint not." Understand that the promises of God are not something you will ever have to worry about, if He said it, He will do it…Glory!

In the sandpaper phase the grit, or size of the granules on the paper, will decrease as the number increases, so an 80-grit sheet is more coarse then a 120 grit. Sand is no longer used on the paper, but different types of minerals and abrasives. For the purposes of sharpening a metal blade you have to be sure to get a type of paper that will do the job. Not all abrasives are tough enough to get the job done, so sometimes the best thing for you is the thing that rubs you the hardest. Too many times in the development of the man, he will choose the easier softer way and that will always yield a mediocre outcome, nothing ventured nothing gained.

In the process of sanding, the blade is rubbed against the paper in a way to remove any of the excess roughage left by the whetstone. Like the whetstone a lubricant is applied to the paper to ease the friction, but for the sandpaper phase, water is suggested and as we know that water is used to symbolize the blood of Christ in the process of the baptism and that blood will continue to sooth the saint. Only under the cover of the blood can we accomplish the goal of the Master and therefore the blood will always apply. By applying the water to the paper, the dust and debris produced in the process is minimized. The blood or water applied to the paper implies that the person being used as the abrasive needs to be truly covered in the Christ…a saved man of God. Sometimes the saint will look outside of the faith for direction and find himself lost in a worldly view of a situation that sounds good but is not congruent with the Word. The Bible teaches in Proverbs 3:5 Trust in the LORD with all thine heart; and lean not unto thine own understanding. Proverbs 3:6 In all thy ways acknowledge him, and he shall direct thy paths. Proverbs 14:12

There is a way which seemeth right unto a man, but the end thereof are the ways of death.

As the blade is rubbed back and forth against the paper the blade becomes increasingly, sharp. Again, the direction of the force comes from the perspective of the blade to the paper, or the perspective of the person having to do the work. Yes, the sandpaper has to be chosen correctly to be able to accomplish the job, but the person being sharpened has to be willing to do the heavy lifting.

At Greater Grace God has revealed many people at many times to take me deeper into the revelation of His Will for my life, but the most powerful experiences or lessons have not been so easily taught. God used the director of the Greeters to rub out my hostile disposition;(I was coming to the Church and did not really know why, what I did know was that I did not want to keep living the way I was living, and I did not know how to change. I was cut off from the human experience and did not really know how to communicate when it was not about the life I was coming from, but Brother Art just kept pushing his way into my life, inviting me to be a part of his committee and correcting me when my approach was a little tart to the new member, and before you know it not only did I know them…but they knew me.)

God used a childhood rival to rub out judgmentalism and to teach me true brotherly love.(In a time of high worship I was thrust together with brother Deon who I only knew at this point from being this arrogant know it all from the south end who had a chip on his shoulder and I knew there was nothing wholly about him, but God stepped in and instructed Bishop to assign me and Deon together to represent the Brotherhood and I would go on to watch God use him to build a fellowship and to push me into another level of functioning. Deon believed in me when I did not believe in myself and continued to push me, demonstrating that even with an edge God is Love…He taught me the importance of prayer and standing in the Gap for your children and how to truly trust and depend on a friend)

God used the Elders and Pastor's to rub out condemnation and to teach holiness, (As I came to the alter week after week with issues of the flesh, having sex, cussing, struggling with pornography, feeling less than, beginning to see spiritually, struggling with my being called of God, my being able to stand in the Gap for and intercede to my being able to fight off attacks of Satan no matter what the issue or situation the Elder's and Pastors connected with me and pushed, pulled or shoved me into the solution God showed them for me.)

He used the Youth Ministry to rub out the delusions of grandeur and to expand my horizons, (The children are our future and their sense of decrement is unlike any other faction of the Church, I quickly learned that God can use a child to teach me and to correct me, I was able to understand that regardless of what I felt about my abilities God did and does flow in and through me. They trusted me we grew together)

God used and uses the Sunday School Ministry to rub out arrogance. (I quickly learned that when you study to teach God teaches you first through the lesson He gives you to teach and only with an open mind and humble spirit can you truly be effective in Him)

God used Mother Dennis and the Tarry Ministry to rub out doubt, yes sometimes brothers the right particle on the paper is a woman, (As I learned the significance of yielding to the Spirit to allow God to flow through You and into others all doubt has been erased, I have seen deaf ears open, demons cast out, children freed and homes restored through the power of His touch. I learned that when God assigns you to a person's life that you are attached until God says different.)

God used the Baptismal Ministry to rub out fear (As I was able to be a part of the birthing of souls into the kingdom of God, I have learned that in that position I am truly an ambassador of God and there is no room for hesitation or fear. I have come head to head with Satan and through the Power of God been able to set the captive free.)

God has and is using the Brotherhood Ministry to rub out discouragement and to expand my faith. (I have learned that the reason we are fought the hardest is because we are the head and only when we acknowledge our true position will we ever experience the true freedom and power that He has for us.)

God has used my employment experiences to shape and direct and the education process to reveal Himself even clearer in the miracle He did in my life. (From the very first adult drug free job at the Deli, God has shown Himself to be a miracle worker, working on my behalf, granting me favor in the sights of them all and using each work situation to develop different parts of my character.

In college God showed me just How Bad He is…ever biological book I read about the human physiology of addiction, it continued to confirm over and over that I should not be able to function at a normal level of intelligence and that there is no way in man's understanding that I would be able to achieve a Master's degree…but here we stand God and I proven them wrong).

God used and uses Elder, Pastor, Bishop Logan to rub out imperfections in my character and to prepare me for His Purpose. (Bishop Logan is God's voice He chose to assign to my life and through him…he teaches, equips, empowers and proves me. I came in the door weak, broken and defeated and today stand strong in the confidence of the faith, unwavering and un-movable-Christ is the God and He did Create everything that was Created and without Him nothing exists. He did live a life for real and did suffer the shame of the crucifixion and did die for my sin's and was buried and did on the third day rise from the dead and has reclaimed my soul from the clutches of hell. There is none other Name Under Heaven whereby I must be saved. I believe in the baptism in the only name of Jesus for the remission of sins and I firmly believe that He does come and live on the inside of man in the form of the Holy Spirit and one form of evidence confirming that conversion is the speaking in tongues as His Spirit Gives Utterance. He will always provide an opportunity for growth and the sandpaper process will forever be available. He tells me Choose Ye Daily Who You Will Serve, and Today I Choose You Lord.

Chapter 2

Countenance is defined in the Strong's Hebrew Dictionary, as:

Countenance = 6440 = paniym paw-neem'

plural (but always as singular) of an unused noun (paneh {paw-neh'}; from 6437); **the face (as the part that turns)**; used in a great variety of applications (literally and figuratively); also (with prepositional prefix) as a preposition (before, etc.):--+ accept, a-(be-)fore(-time), against, anger, X as (long as), at, + battle, + because (of), + beseech, countenance, edge, + **employ, endure, + enquire, face, favor, fear of, for, forefront(-part), form**(-er time, -ward), from, front, heaviness, X **him(-self),** + honorable, + impudent, + in, it, look(-eth) (- s), X **me**, + meet, X more than, mouth, of, off, (of) old (time), X on, open, + **out of, over against, the partial, person**, + please, presence, propect, was purposed, by reason of, + regard, right forth, + serve, X shewbread, sight, state, straight, + street, X thee, X them(-selves**), through (+ - out), till, time(-s) past, (un-)to(-ward), + upon, upside (+ down), with(- in, + -stand), X ye, X you.**

6437 = panah paw-naw'

a primitive root; to turn; by implication, to face, i.e. appear, look, etc.:--appear, at (even-)tide, behold, cast out, come on, X corner, dawning, empty, go away, lie, look, mark, pass away, prepare, regard, (have) respect (to), (re-)turn (aside, away, back, face, self), X right (early).

Countenance is a plural but always singular in reference to the triune nature of man, spirit, soul and body as a plural that operate in the singular. It is the face as the part of a man that turns or changes as the situation changes, it will look different depending on the experiences of the individual there is a look for everything that we experience. A look of endurance to go through a look of relief after you come through, but often times we have the look of heaviness as we deal with.

Every outer expression is tied to an inner experience, so the outward appearance of a man is more than facial expression; it is an external representation of an emotional and spiritual experience that is most oftentimes representative of the actual essence or soul of the person. Our everyday experience shape who we become, and who we become changes as we grow through those experiences.

Countenance: 1. appearance, especially the look or expression of the face: *a sad countenance.*

2. the face; visage.
3. calm facial expression; composure.
4. approval or favor; encouragement; moral support.
5. *Obsolete.* bearing; behavior.

countenance. (n.d.). *Dictionary.com Unabridged*. Retrieved December 13, 2013, from Dictionary.com website: http://dictionary.reference.com/browse/countenance

The Hebrew word for Countenance is paw-neem' coming from the root word paw-naw' which means to face i.e. appear to look at, appear at, behold, cast out, come on, empty, prepare, regard, have respect to, return face, return self.

That unlocks the parable of the sharpening process that requires a file, a wetstone and some sandpaper. Iron is a soft metal and cannot in fact sharpen itself; it requires another harder metal to become sharp. But the Proverb said that Iron sharpeneth Iron does the word of God lie??? Of course, not the truth is in so a man sharpeneth or bring into clarity, the countenance, the "external representation of emotional and spiritual experience that is most oftentimes representative of the actual essence or soul of the person"....the whole man. This is a harder process to sharpen, the self, the image, the heart of another. But it is not the mere similarities of the fact that a man is the same as a man, Men are different types of strength or hardness in and of themselves. In order for you to fully grab the concept of the hardness or strength of another you have to have a God-view, not man-view of who you truly are.

The Bible says in Genesis that He, God made man in His Image. Genesis 1:26 And God said, let **us** make man in our image, after our likeness: and let them have dominion over the fish of the sea, and over the fowl of the air, and over the cattle, and over all the earth, and over every creeping thing that creepeth upon the earth.

See when I know my original design it is much easier to form a self-opinion of where I am in relationship to where I think I am supposed to be. Too often instead of understanding that I was created to have dominion I walk as if I am inferior too. Understanding who you are will better allow you to appreciate the strength or hardness of others. If you see someone walking in a place that you believe you are called to be or capable of being and you are not there, then that person has the appropriate hardness to add acuteness to your self-view in that area.

In the beginning God had an intention for the image of man that was perfect. We were determined to be exactly what He wanted us to be we were created to worship Him, but even before the idea of worship is introduced in this process let's look at His original design for us. In the Beginning God!!!! God was before anything He existed because He did and in and of Himself, He is complete. Attempting to fully describe the origin of God is impossible for man; in His Word in Isaiah 55:8-9, He states that His ways are higher than our ways and His thoughts are not the same as our thoughts but we so foolishly attempt to capture the true nature of God in comparison to the finiteness of His creation which is us, which is Adam in his singleness as a individual and in the totality of Adam which is all mankind.

Isaiah 55:8 For my thoughts are not your thoughts, neither are your ways my ways, saith the LORD.

Isaiah 55:9 For as the heavens are higher than the earth, so are my ways higher than your ways, and my thoughts than your thoughts.

Knowing our original design will unlock your self-awareness of your true potential. Man was created so magnificently that Adam was assigned the task of identifying and labeling every other living creature on the planet. True dominion gives privilege and true sonship gives honor.

Having the wisdom to name and categorize a species that has never been seen by man before is in itself amazing, but to be able to do it in a way that has proven to be what we now know as scientifically significant is miraculous. There are those of us today that are driven by that original creativeness and continue to search the face of the earth for unknown life forms or I should say forgotten or unfamiliar life forms and they tap into that original creative energy of our first selves Adam to be able to bring to the worlds awareness a newly named creature or species that he or she can claim Adamic credit for.

Naming a newly discovered creature in today's time is actually only tapping into a cosmic place of man's remembrance of his original assignment from God to have true dominion. Even in those unfettered individuals who seem to have embraced their life's purpose there is always someone who went before that was able to participate in the process of sharpening, but knowing your true calling or purpose produces what is commonly thought of as a glow.

The term glow is often used to express the outward projection of a self-actualized countenance. But true self-actualization or "the achievement of one's full potential through creativity, independence, spontaneity, and a grasp of the real world." *Dictionary.com Unabridged*. Retrieved March 2, 2018 from

Dictionary.com website http://www.dictionary.com/browse/self-actualization" is only realized when we learn to surrender to the call of God in our lives.

God said that all things are possible to him that believe, the possibility of the realization of real self-actualization, actually depends on you allowing yourself to see yourself through the Eyes of God. God has a plan for You and His plan was imprinted on our spirits and waits for us to unlock our destiny.

Attempting to relocate the image of self-intended by God is often times a journey and that journey is called life. As you grow through the process there will be many presented that have the ability to assist with your experience but determining the hardness of the tool is sometimes difficult, and just like clay in the hands of God if you allow an inappropriate tool to be applied to your process you will have to return to the master for remolding more times than intended.

Being aware of the plan for man or Adam is one thing but being able to carry it out is the journey. Remember God spoke into the darkness and called the light forward…the light was already in existence in the darkness but was not aware of its power to shine until ignited by the Word of God coming from the Voice of God. Gen 1:2-5. See when you are in the process of being made, make sure that you seek the Face of God first for direction. Many men will see and say things to and about you that might sound good, but do they sound God?

When Moses was placed in the cleft of the rock to be exposed to the mere presence of the backside of God, he came out with such a glow that the countenance of his face had to be hidden from the people by a veil. Ex 33:21-3. God's presence will always cause you to be different, and just because others that you were once familiar with are not comfortable with the glow of God in your life doesn't mean that what you are now doing is wrong.

Moses was able to put a veil over his face to protect the people from his newly acquired brilliance, but he was not able to not fulfill God's purpose in his life. God will allow you to make provision, not excuses.

The Bible teaches that there are those who are called of God and equipped by God with his supernatural knowledge of a skill that were instructed to teach; Be careful believing that you can learn all you need to know about a subject from your experience. Ex 35:31-4. The sharpening process of brotherhood will take you to places that you cannot get to on your own. The closer you come to God the brighter your continence with shine. When seeking to please God to fulfill His purpose becomes your true internal motivation then the external expression to others can only be perceived as His glow.

Chapter Three

The Stages of Manhood becoming God Centered

There are many books written on the topic of manhood, which tend to describe it from many different scientific positions. The Bible starts this topic off with more of a charge, in Corinthians God admonishes us to change the internal perceptions of some common everyday events as we transition into what we call manhood. First Corinthians 13:11states "When I was a child, I spoke as a child, I understood as a child, I thought as a child: but when I became a man, I put away childish things."

In our society it is common to be more patient with people when we feel like they have not been appropriately trained in a skill or situation. That level of patience is amplified in our allowances to our children. Children are not expected to understand some of the things they do as being wrong the first time they encounter them. The first time your child approaches the electric socket you panic because of their inability to comprehend the danger that is connected to the shiny object on the wall. After the all so familiar teaching tone of Aah Aah, we are even subject to as adults to jump over furniture to prevent our children from electrocuting themselves. Even with all of the socket covers and rearranging of furniture to prevent them access, there are not too many children who do not still get zapped by the outlet.

The first time our son or daughter is in a emotional relationship, try as we may, we are not able to stop the heartache of the break-up, after a while just like with the outlet, we expect them to be able to make better choices based on the negative reinforcement caused by the pain of the previous experience. The Bible appears to have an entirely different approach to the subject of manhood. We are instructed to as men to, "put away" or to stop participating in behaviors that are "childish". The problem for most is that the true understanding of childish is not clearly stated or even explained.

In the text the word for child and childish both come from the same Greek word "nhpioV; nepios; nay'-pee-os" which means "not speaking…i.e. and infant (minor); figuratively, a simple-minded person, an immature Christian" (Strong's Greek Dictionary). This connotation of not speaking a word, takes us to the actual instructions of the verse which deals with speech. "Spake as a child" the process of becoming a man in this since is tied directly to the things that you allow to come out of your mouth. You become known by the reputation that you carry, and that reputation is directly connected to your speech.

The Bible in Matthew says, "for out of the abundance of the heart the mouth speaketh" (Mt 12:34). See the charge that God is giving Men as it relates to manhood is to guard your heart, if you guard your heart and keep it connected to the Word of God then those things that you find yourself speaking will more likely be in line with what God would have you say. Immaturity in the Word will cause shipwreck and that is the stages of manhood that I will be addressing in this chapter.

The order of the verse states that we spake, we understood, we thought which illustrates the adult process backwards. As an adult you should have a thought that drives your understanding that should be able to guide the things you speak, but as a child we spake out of the limited experiences of childhood. There is a common saying in our culture, I am not sure where it originated but you hear it often said, "out of the mouths of babes" that sometimes is used to describe a statement of truth spoken by a young person that should not be able to truly understand the extent of the situation." See if we develop a steady diet of the Word of God and time spent in the presence of God in prayer and meditation, then those things that God has for you will be more easily accessible.

The Bible teaches us in Proverbs 3:5 "Trust in the LORD with all thine heart; and lean not unto thine own understanding. As children we tend to lean on the understanding of the environment. When we are scared, we fight or run, when we are ashamed, we hide or fight, when we are hungry we eat and when we are blind we are lost. Naturally these are the reactions of the fleshly man to the fleshly experiences. The Apostle Paul gave example that despite the thorn in his flesh which he says was given to him and he also prayed for God to remove, he identifies in II Corinthians, that it is that exact infirmity that has revealed the awesomeness of God. God tells him that His, "God's" grace is sufficient and that it is in the infirmities of man that God is made strong. Paul teaches that it is that an honor to be afflicted for the sake of the ministry.

See this is significant because in the life of a believer of Christ the adversary, satan will always be on the attack, if satan is not attacking you then you are probably doing what he is at least okay with you doing if you are not in fact doing his bidding weather consciously or unconsciously. No I am not saying that if a man is scared he should not fight, but what I am saying is if a man is in a situation that would normally spark a reaction of fear that instead of him responding to the fleshly experience with a fleshly reaction that as he matures he should be more apt to respond with a Godly reaction.

If I know that God "Christ" is not the author of fear and I know that Greater is He that is in Me than he that is in the World, and I know that All things work together for good of the called than why would I ever be afraid. If I believe that All things are possible to him who believes and that without Christ nothing exist then why would I doubt. If I believe that man should not live on bread alone but on every Word that proceedeth out of the Mouth of God than why would I hunger.

Spiritual reactions to natural situations are a true sign of manhood. Christ says a man should love his wife as Christ loved the Church. That means being willing to lay down his life for his wife. If you are not ready for that level of a commitment than you are not ready to be a husband, and you are not ready to be involved with a woman in the way that leads to marriage. Too many men put the cart before the horse and fall in lust with the woman before falling in Love with God. The Love of God will guide you into position and provide you with the ability to love a woman.

The Bible teaches that the man is the head of the family and too often headship is interpreted as dominator. Christ led the people of God by example, He did not expect us to do anything that He did not do first, He does not expect you to give anything that He did not give You first. Yes everything exist because and for Him, but personal relationship with God has personal privilege. God Honors those who Honor Him. As a man we take our leadership from God, all will follow as You follow Christ and true headship is just that. When the Spirit of God leads You then and only then are you qualified to lead others.

As a Father it is your responsibility to train up your children in the ways of God, and His Word promises that they will not depart from that. Job prayed for his children daily for sins they might have knowingly or unknowingly committed as a covering. Father's cover their children, they guide their children, they provide for their children and yes in times of need they chastise their children. The

Bible teaches that God chastens those who he loves and we too often times in today's culture vilify the need to chastise the child.

The Bible goes as far to teach the benefits of spanking a child can be as significant as delivering his soul from hell! Spanking is not the goal of parenting but is sometimes required. Too often in today's can't we all just get along society or, children have the right to choose craziness, we forget that children think, reason, understand and speak as children and it is the responsibility of the Father to lead.

When I became a man, I put away childish things, those things that sustained our youth and were only possible because of the input of elders are childish things. The key that unlocks the concept of childish things for me is those things that we come to understand as we mature into adulthood that we took for granted as children. We did not understand the cost of the turning up the thermostat in the winter but were oh so willing to do it when our parents weren't looking and could not fully conceive of the concept in our limited ability of why it was wrong to do because it just made since.

We did not understand that as the person responsible for paying the bills certain things had to be taken into consideration when determining the best confront level the family could afford. Something as simple as turning up the thermostat a few degrees was difference for most in having the ability to afford new shoes for the entire family or having to eat hamburger instead of steak.

Childish things are those want driven desires that sometimes just were not possible due to the needs of the environment. You hear many stories of how Momma scraped food off her plate to feed the children, but what is often missed in that picture is that image of the man who is out of the house at dinner time earning the little bit of money that the family has. Putting away childish things means not being willing to allow this image to be perpetuated by our society.

You as a man are not insignificant You are needed, Your presence in the family is a must and You are the only one that can fully change the image of man that sometimes even you possess.

Standing up to take your rightful place in the system as a whole is putting away childish things. You have to be willing to accept the level of responsibility that comes along with the activity of the pleasures of sex. If you are not willing to be what she needs, what they need, what is required then put away the childish desire to please just your flesh. It is a childish image that says you can have the relationship with her without being what she needs you to be.

Love is something that doesn't just go away; a relationship takes work, and just because it is not fun anymore does not give you the right to run. In all things seek the Face of God; if God guided you to her, fellas, then it is what it is supposed to be. Ladies it is not your job to seek him it is his job to find you. There is an order in God that when applied yields perfection.

As I started out on this journey, I did not really know what to expect, but I knew that God was and is in control. I have for as long as I can remember been someone that others have relied on for support and counsel, even when I at times had neither. As I have stated this far, God has used the various operations in the ministry at Greater Grace Temple to develop me, but at times I was unsure of what I was doing or how effective I was or am being, but in every stage, I have and will continually, sought the face of God in all directional decisions. I say directional decisions because I cannot honestly say that I have always taken the time to ask direction before making every decision, but I can honestly say that I have not moved from one place to another without consulting God first.

Being involved with the Brotherhood of GGT has been an ever-changing experience that has just recently come to life in its meaning for this purpose. From attending what was known simply to me as the Brotherhood under the first director, to become what we called Boys to Men under another Director that developed into and along with the vision of the house with the constant them coined by Bishop Logan of Iron Sharpens Iron, that come to be known under my leadership as the Men of Grace, the fellowship with our brothers has remained a constant. See as I prayerfully write about the stages of Manhood as I have titled them, I had to first experience the fallacies and experiences of the Men of Grace in order to fully appreciate my own.

"Thought as a child" see I used to operate under the impression that I had to first experience things to be able to learn from the experience, but God has guided me to a well of experience to draw from that I didn't even know was happening until it was happening, but in all fairness He always had a plan.

As a young man I grew up without the guidance of my biological father who was in prison for most of my life, but God always provided a ram in the bush. There was always a male figure in my life that had my back. My Grandfather's both concrete workers taught me the value of hard work, and how to love and provide for a woman. My neighborhood male leaders who motivated me to do better by holding me accountable and correcting me when I was in the streets were at that time viewed as meddlesome, but I can see now the hand of God even then guiding me out of harm's way. The school teachers over the years who all pitched in at different times to encourage me to become more than I thought I could, and even like Joseph I found grace and favor and grew positively in jails, prison and judicial sanction systems that I became involved in, "Understood as a child".

Being thrust into the care of the mishmash molly toss group of Men that only God could have drawn together was where I truly learned to appreciate the awesomeness of God's favor and the power of His might. Coming together we began to trust each other, there were times that we took turns telling each other what we believed was our unique testimonies. But the more we met the clearer and clearer the picture developed that God provides exactly what you need when you need it every time.

It is not easy to get men to commit to come together, but as Bishop Logan always teaches, as the head goes the body will follow. I was not always the head of the brotherhood of GGT but I did notice in my involvement that it is the leader that sets the tone, but over the years every time we develop, connect and broke down and re-connected the theme has remained the same, Men need Men to develop and more importantly Saved Men need other Saved Men to grow in Christ. Yes, yes, yes I know Christ can do anything He wants, to whomever He wants, whenever He wants and does not need our permission to do it, but we are not Christ and we do need each other to grow. It might have been the Mothers that loved me into trust, but it was the Brothers that taught me practical application.

I thought I was the only one who was blood washed fire baptized and Holy Ghost filled who also found it at times impossible to quiet the flesh, "Spake as a Child". I used to think that I was weak, or possibly so demonically immoral that even the Holy Ghost couldn't fix. Coming from a lifestyle of sexual immorality, drug use, criminal activity and poverty, it at times felt to overwhelming. I would be in the midst of prayer and be overtaken by lust for everything from my past.

I would walk out of a service where I witnessed the miracles of God that could not be doubted, for example I saw a leg grown, a tumor chased down a arm and dissolved in the hands of the person praying, I have witnessed demons jumping from the bodies of people, only to walk out of that service and go home and masturbate to porn. I would ask myself how can I be who they say that I am, the minister, elder, pastor, and man of God and that question lingered at every stage of development until I was able to understand that it was not what they said that matters but it was what God said to me that matters.

I have asked myself did He call me to be a minister or was I just being full of myself, did He call me to advance to the office of Elder or was it because I am a good student, did He elevate me to Pastor or was I a convenient fill in because everyone else has left the Church, Did he call me to be a Man of God or is that even real. See at every level there is a new level of doubt that I had to overcome, but with the help, experience and love of the Men of Grace the Voice of God is amplified through them, and I can say Yes to everything God has said that I am.

I won't start mentioning names of who did or said what because over the years I am sure to forget or possibly offend many. From the very beginning Men have poured out their experience with church to help us get a better relationship with self to be able to push through the experience of church. What I mean by church in this statement is the place where we gather more so than the reality of Church actually being the true Body of Christ and what all that means, but we grow. When the brothers discussed their past frustrations with being looked over by elders or being called on out of need for their skills and not out of direction from God or their perception of such, helped others see that their perception of events was not a sign of weakness but an actual attack of satan.

When I heard other brothers discuss how they took drugs and functioned in high levels of professionalism or ministry then I knew that I was not alone in my struggle despite my drug use being prior to me having any status or position. When I heard the testimony of men who struggled with sex, image, status, honor, ego and just about every sin I can think of and who also had past experiences of abuse, rape, incarceration, drug addiction, poverty and immorality and were all able to still praise God…then I started to believe. See it was not in their fallacies or failures that I found strength or identification; it was in their Praise that I found freedom. Yes, they at times had fallen short, yes, they at times had doubted self, yes they at times had not been what they wanted to be, but in all that they went through they still had and have a Praise on their lips.

I had to start of teaching the kids in pre-school and kindergarten for years to get an understanding and experience with the innocence of God. I had to be involved with and lead the Baptism ministry to get and understanding and experience of the birthing process and the war room protocols. I had to be involved with the youth department during its development of the vision of 1615 "But who do you say that I am" in order to understand the complexities of honor, love, respect and dedication. I had to be on the counseling staff to understand the importance of applying the Word to every, everyday situation as a compass to prevent shipwreck. I thank God for being able to be of service in the cleaning of the building, the feeding of the hungry ministry, the drug and alcohol outreach endeavors to help me understand the strengths of my experience.

Becoming a Shepherd, Servant Leader, Pastor has been required of God and is required of God for the servicing of His flock, but for me it is also required to teach me true love. God first opened me to this concept when he gifted me with a son…even out of wedlock and in a state of complete immoral debauchery; God introduced me to His Love. He teaches us that No Greater Love is there than a man to lay down his life for a friend. Christ lived the example of that love in his Crucifixion, Burial and Resurrection, but He first showed me His Love through the life He gifted me with in my son.

I thought I had loved my Grandma, my Mom, my Siblings, them whoever them was, but none of those feelings compared to the feeling I had when I realized the reality of fatherhood. I loved my son from the moment of awareness of his conception to this day and that was only a glimpse of the Love that I felt when I was first overshadowed and then in-filled with the Holly Ghost. Being Called to be His Pastor and an extension of Him to His flock can only be described in our vocabulary as Awesome. But only through the support guidance and love of others are we able to withstand and preserver in His mission.

It's not about me, but it's all about me. Ask yourself what concept or belief do you have about yourself that is not of God? How important is it, and where did it come from? What God has for You is for You, but those things that you were connected to in one phase of the walk were only meant to be used for that period.

God has a plan for Your Life that is dependent on Your willingness to follow through with becoming the adult version of You. Who told you that…whatever that is? God said a man born of a woman is but a few days and full of trouble, Job 14.1. What will your trouble feel like, will you stay connected to the immature expectations of your flesh or will You walk in the fullness of Who God Called You to Be?

Putting away childish things…in conclusion I pray that you touch with me in this prayer as I as We go to the next level of manhood in God…the stages of Manhood never stop we are always a work in progress.

Father God touch the reader of this prayer, open his mind to Your call in his life, if it be in the hand of a sinner, *forgive him, and allow him to pray this prayer of faith, Father God forgive me of all sin both known and unknown, I believe in Your Life, Death Burial and Resurrection, Jesus I surrender to You today as My Lord and Savior.*

If it be in the hands of one sent by the adversary to learn Your ways to snare Your children, *Grab Him Father and touch his heart penetrate his spirit and reclaim his soul, save him today.*

If it be in the hand of one of Your children that You have guided to connect with me then *cover him forgive and keep us in oneness take us to another level in You, prepare us to be the Men that You have intended for Us to be, Pour out Your Spirit in Us and thrust Us into a place of effectiveness in You. Protect those that are near and dear to our hearts and grant Us access into the Inner Place in You where no enemies dwell. We thank You for each other today, We, Your children thank You for the opportunity to Serve You, show Us Our true Worth in You. As Men we touch and Agree right now that By Your Stripes We are Healed and that No Weapon Formed Against Us will Prosper. We thank You right now for Our new-found revelation of Your intention for Us and We Surrender to Your Will...Father Use Us...In Jesus Name We Pray Amen.*

Other Biblical Reference Used but not directly included in the Text:

Genesis 1:26 And God said, Let **us** make man in our image, after our likeness: and let them have dominion over the fish of the sea, and over the fowl of the air, and over the cattle, and over all the earth, and over every creeping thing that creepeth upon the earth.

Genesis 1:27 So God created man in his own image, in the image of God created he him; male and female created he them.

Genesis 1:28 And God blessed them, and God said unto them, Be fruitful, and multiply, and replenish the earth, and subdue it: and have dominion over the fish of the sea, and over the fowl of the air, and over every living thing that moveth upon the earth.

Genesis 2:7 And the LORD God formed man of the dust of the ground and breathed into his nostrils the breath of life; and man became a living soul.

Genesis 2:19 And out of the ground the LORD God formed every beast of the field, and every fowl of the air; and brought them unto Adam to see what he would call them: and whatsoever Adam called every living creature, that was the name thereof.

Genesis 2:20 And Adam gave names to all cattle, and to the fowl of the air, and to every beast of the field; but for Adam there was not found an help meet for him.

Genesis 2:21 And the LORD God caused a deep sleep to fall upon Adam, and he slept: and he took one of his ribs, and closed up the flesh instead thereof;

Genesis 2:22 And the rib, which the LORD God had taken from man, made he a woman, and brought her unto the man.

Genesis 2:23 And Adam said, This is now bone of my bones, and flesh of my flesh: she shall be called Woman, because she was taken out of Man.

Genesis 5:3 And Adam lived an hundred and thirty years, and begat a son in his own likeness, after his image; and called his name Seth:

Exodus 33:21 And the LORD said, Behold, there is a place by me, and thou shalt stand upon a rock:

Exodus 33:22 And it shall come to pass, while my glory passeth by, that I will put thee in a clift of the rock, and will cover thee with my hand while I pass by:

Exodus 33:23 And I will take away mine hand, and thou shalt see my back parts: but my face shall not be seen.

Exodus 35:31 And he hath filled him with the spirit of God, in wisdom, in understanding, and in knowledge, and in all manner of workmanship;

Exodus 35:32 And to devise curious works, to work in gold, and in silver, and in brass,

Exodus 35:33 And in the cutting of stones, to set them, and in carving of wood, to make any manner of cunning work.

Exodus 35:34 And he hath put in his heart that he may teach, both he, and Aholiab, the son of Ahisamach, of the tribe of Dan.

Proverbs 3:5 Trust in the LORD with all thine heart; and lean not unto thine own understanding.

Proverbs 23:13 Withhold not correction from the child: for if thou beatest him with the rod, he shall not die.

Proverbs 23:14 Thou shalt beat him with the rod, and shalt deliver his soul from hell.

Matthew 12:34 O generation of vipers, how can ye, being evil, speak good things? for out of the abundance of the heart the mouth speaketh.

1 Corinthians 1:27 But God hath chosen the foolish things of the world to confound the wise; and God hath chosen the weak things of the world to confound the things which are mighty;

2 Corinthians 12:9 And he said unto me, My grace is sufficient for thee: for my strength is made perfect in weakness. Most gladly therefore will I rather glory in my infirmities, that the power of Christ may rest upon me.

2 Corinthians 12:10 Therefore I take pleasure in infirmities, in reproaches, in necessities, in persecutions, in distresses for Christ's sake: for when I am weak, then am I strong.

Revelation 3:19 As many as I love, I rebuke and chasten: be zealous therefore, and repent.

Bibliography

sharpen. (n.d.). *Collins English Dictionary - Complete & Unabridged 10th Edition*. Retrieved February 05, 2014, from Dictionary.com website:
http://dictionary.reference.com/browse/sharpen

sharp. (n.d.). *Dictionary.com Unabridged*. Retrieved February 05, 2014, from Dictionary.com website:
http://dictionary.reference.com/browse/sharp

William, J. (Demand Media, 1994-2014). *ehow:process of iron sharpening*. Retrieved from http://www.ehow.com/how-does_5611896_process-iron-sharpening.html

About.com. *How To Sharpen a Knife With a Whetstone*. Retrieved 9/29/14, from
http://culinaryarts.about.com/od/knivescutlery/ht/whetstone.htm

Sharpening Stone. (n.d.). *Wikipeda-The Free Encyclopedia*, Retrieved September 29, 2014, from website:
http://en.wikipedia.org/wiki/Sharpening_stone

whet. (n.d.). *Collins English Dictionary - Complete & Unabridged 10th Edition*. Retrieved September 29, 2014, from Dictionary.com website: http://dictionary.reference.com/browse/whet

stone. (n.d.). *Dictionary.com Unabridged*. Retrieved September 29, 2014, from Dictionary.com website:
http://dictionary.reference.com/browse/stone

http://www.wikihow.com/Sharpen-Kitchen-Knives-with-Sandpaper, Retrieved June 9, 2015

http://www.stumpynubs.com/assets/sharpening-grit-chart-2.pdf, Retrieved June 11, 2015

self-actualization. (n.d.). *Dictionary.com Unabridged.* Retrieved March 2, 2018 from Dictionary.com website http://www.dictionary.com/browse/self-actualization

Other titles from Higher Ground Books & Media:

Wise Up to Rise Up by Rebecca Benston

A Path to Shalom by Steen Burke

Overcomer by Forrest Henslee

Miracles: I Love Them by Forest Godin

32 Days with Christ's Passion by Mark Etter

Knowing Affliction and Doing Recovery by John Baldasare

Out of Darkness by Stephen Bowman

Healing in God's Power by Yvonne Green

The Tin Can Gang by Chuck David

I Don't Want to Be Like You by Maryanne Christiano-Mistretta

Add these titles to your collection today!

http://www.highergroundbooksandmedia.com

www.ingramcontent.com/pod-product-compliance
Lightning Source LLC
Chambersburg PA
CBHW020019050426
42450CB00005B/550